# Butterfly With A Broken Wing

by

## Renfroe Edward Watson, Jr.

Bloomington, IN  Milton Keynes, UK

authorHOUSE®

*AuthorHouse™*
*1663 Liberty Drive, Suite 200*
*Bloomington, IN 47403*
*www.authorhouse.com*
*Phone: 1-800-839-8640*

*AuthorHouse™ UK Ltd.*
*500 Avebury Boulevard*
*Central Milton Keynes, MK9 2BE*
*www.authorhouse.co.uk*
*Phone: 08001974150*

*First published by AuthorHouse 2/1/2007*

*ISBN: 978-1-4259-7746-7 (e)*
*ISBN: 978-1-4259-7745-0 (sc)*

*Library of Congress Control Number: 2006909950*

*Printed in the United States of America*
*Bloomington, Indiana*

*This book is printed on acid-free paper.*

# BUTTERFLY WITH A BROKEN WING

by

Renfroe Edward Watson, Jr.

cover paintings by

Jon D. Watson

and

Mary Spencer-Watson

# ACKNOWLEDGMENTS AND APPRECIATIONS

Grateful acknowledgment is made to those whose faith has touched my life, many of which live on upon this earth only in the memories of lives enriched: Byron Herbert Reece, whose poetic love of creation birthed a love of poetry in my spirit; The Reverend Hubert Dodd, whose poems of faith created an awe of faith in my heart; Claude Underwood, who saw God's hand upon this world even in the smallest of creatures. They, and many others, brought life and faith together and made each the more real.

A special appreciation goes to my family: A mother, who gave me a handful of flower seeds and taught me the patience to allow God to grow a Zinnia; a father, who could point to a dead tree and see life; a wife, who allowed me the freedom to sit beneath the boughs and listen to the songs of God; and three children, each with the artistic ability to capture on canvas the miracles of the Creator.

And finally, thanks to Jon, our son, who created the butterfly for this book's cover and to Mary, our daughter-in-law, for the back painting.

# DEDICATION

This little book is dedicated to those who have taught me the most and those whom I have loved the deepest: Phyllis, my beloved wife

Fred, deceased, who had an abiding love for God's creation

And Jon and David, both talented, able and caring sons.

# TABLE OF CONTENTS

# PREFACE

He fluttered about upon the breeze, that beautiful butterfly. When he fell to the ground with a broken wing, I knew he had been sent just for me. Our eldest son had died after a long and heartbreaking illness, and I had struggled for words to express the moment. I knew, then, that it is pain that often draws humanity together. We all have pains, and we all struggle to comprehend the moment and feel the faith to carry on.

For years, I have sat alone to think and pray during the early hours of each day to find the words, to share the words, of faith with others. Often those words have found their way into Sunday messages and printed newsletters and, now, into this little book.

One evening, lying upon the ground in a sleeping bag, I was sung to sleep by the beautiful voice of a bird to the west. The next morning, still lying there, I heard the song again, this time from the distant east. As the sun arose, the song grew nearer until it seemed to sound above my head. Had I remained long enough, I am sure it would have again faded to the west.

I imagined that song had encircled the earth to find its way to my ears. When and where did it start? Alas, in ancient days, somewhere some bird had sung the notes and taught them to her children. Then, the children had taught them to their children, until across the world - around the world - the song was sung. Whence it had started, I knew not. But this I did know, the song was now both received and sent - it had come to me, and it would pass through me to others.

These poems come from lives that have touched mine. They are not mine, for they were given by friends and unknown strangers, by the faithful and the struggling, the silent and the loud, the strong and the week. They have been given, and, oh, how I love to pass them on. Enjoy!

# FLOWERS FOR THE LIVING

*Some call it "flowers for the living," but it appears that the best time to show love, thanksgiving and encouragement is today, while those we thank and love are alive!*

Upon the heart, the words were kept!
Upon the lips, were left unspoken.
Though felt with heat of fervent fire,
Embrace and smile, their only token.

And when the world cried, "'Tis too late.
The life you loved has now been taken,"
Tis the sorrow keenest felt;
Too long the words had been forsaken.

And bending near the deafened ear,
You break the silence long unbroken
And pray that now in heaven's bliss,
She'll hear the words you left unspoken.

And this we find across the age,
That many hearts hath been broken
When love was felt and never spoken.

# THERE WERE TEARS
# IN THE GARDEN

*The hymnist wrote: "I come to the garden alone while the*
*dew is still on the roses..." and there, he met with God.*

In a Garden named Gethsemane
Where gnarled olives grew,
He knelt and prayed in anguish
The holy darkness through.
And there He stained the garden stone
And wept His garden tear,
Surrendered there His will to God
Where only God could hear.

In a Garden near a Hebrew tomb
Where springtime flowers grew,
She yearned to see the one she loved,
The one she barely knew.
And as she wept her garden tear,
A gardener soon drew near.
"Weep not, my friend," He spoke to her.
"The one you seek is here."

In a garden in a private place
Where beautiful flowers grow,
Where birds may sing their lovely songs,
There, pray-ers often go,
They weep a garden tear alone
When no one else is near,
And long to hear those words again,
"The one you seek is here."

*Everyone needs a place of contemplation and*
*thought, a garden in which to pray,*
*to weep, to laugh, to commune with God.  Some*

2

*call it a "closet" of prayer.  For*
*me that's too confining. I prefer the garden surrounded by reminders of a God*
*still at work - a wonderful place to pray.*

# WHISPER SILENCE

**"In quietness and in confidence shall be
your strength." Isaiah 30:15.**

*There comes a time to be quiet and know God - a time when the sound of
silence is real.*

Silence! Silence! Whisper silence!
And hear a chill fall upon the earth,
And ears that have not heard can hear
For silence is the sound of worth.
It shares a love too sweet for speech
When lovers touch their first caress,
Or when in death alas they part
And silence is the sound of tenderness.

Silence! Silence! Whisper silence!
And hear the heartbreak of broken dreams
For how can words express the hurt,
Defend the pain or yet redeem
The love that falls in disrepair?
Then silence is the sound of hopefulness
When face to face two friends may meet
And sit in silent friendliness.

Silence! Silence! Whisper silence!
And learn the mysteries of God's great store
For ears can hear but part of life,
The heart can hear so much more.
The greatest things cannot be told
By word or sound or common pen,
But hearts can hear if hearts are bold
Enough to hush and hear within.

# THE GREATEST OF THESE IS LOVE

How long is love?
It spans the earth on golden wings.
No length of time can be so great
To halt the freshest breeze it brings
It breathes a joy to human heart
From ages past within the mind.
Rebuilds the strength that once was felt
By tenderest cord of humankind.
No clock or rule can measure love.
No length of time nor span of space
Can gauge or tape the reach of love.
'Tis knowing God; 'Tis known by Grace.

# WHO HEARS MY CRY?

Who hears my faintest cry
Sounded under a lonely moon
And stars that dot the sky?
Who turns His ear toward me
And hears my sadful  moan
And hearing, bears me company?
Who promised long as years endure
To be my friend-at-hand
And grant me love secure?
There is no woman, man nor child
Whom that Love yet denies -
None too good and none too vile.
Who sees me stand beneath that sky
And holds my hand all night?
'Tis God, 'tis God, I testify!

# THIS IS THE DAY THE LORD HAS MADE

How illusive the stages of life
That blow like the wondering sand!
Never, it seems, the stage we prefer
Is the stage we have at hand.
As children we dream of being adults,
Anticipate wonderful things.
Adults, then, we dream of being a child
And all of the fun that it brings.
As youth oft' we long to sit retired
Underneath the old apple tree.
Retired, we recall that youth was the day
When the world was so wonderfully free.
How wistfully once we'd sit and we'd wait
'Til life as we dreamed would begin!
How piningly now we wonder at how
To life came so quickly the end.
So, let us take heart wherever we are
Along life's calendar of days.
So definitely true, for fact it is sure
In wonderfully different ways:
The day that we have the nearest at hand
In our lives is the only day.
So live it as full as ever you can,
And use it the best that you may.
For seasons do come, and seasons do go
For all across the great land,
But let it be known, and let it be shared:
The best is the season at hand.


God is sharing His best gift - today!

# TO THE GOD WHO'S THERE

*In a world desperate for help, let's remember that*
*no pain is hidden from God and*
*no hurt beyond His care.*

I've prayed to God by granite stone
Alone, in deep despair.
I've prayed when hurt just wouldn't heal,
And found that God was there.
I've prayed in closet and market place,
On sea and in the air.
I've prayed in field and citadel,
And found that God was there.
I've prayed for friends that I have loved,
For strangers that I've never met.
I've prayed for self, lest I forget
That God is Father, yet.
I've prayed by bed, at table set;
I've prayed while auto bound.
And this I know for this I've found:
God hears the pray-er's sound.
I'll talk with God while there's yet breath,
In victory and despair.
I'll listen, then, to His reply
And know that God doth care.
I'll lift to Him Earth's hurting pain -
Starvation, war, regret,
And know that for this human race
God is the savior, yet.

And I'll say:
What hath You, God, for me to do?
What need must needs be met?
How may I show to all the world
God is the Father, yet?
And how may I reveal the truth
When I complete my prayer
That I have prayed not into space
But to the God already there?

8

# GOD HEARS HIS CHILDREN PRAY

At Chapel rail they knelt to pray
That God's great will be done,
That this, their church, arise to meet
The calling of the Son.
They prayed that we recall the gifts
The saints to us have passed
They prayed that we may pass them on
As long as breath shall last.
'Tis not a simple thing they did,
In simple chapel prayer,`
For such did Abraham bow down,
Then found a lamb ensnared.
And so did Moses lift his voice,
Then raise his arms up high,
And waters parted, divided sea,
As God's redeemed passed by.
And Daniel, in the Lion's lair,
Spoke faithfully also,
And hungry mouths of vicious beasts
Were closed against their foe,
And Jesus in Gethsemane, cried out,
"Thy Will be done..."
And all the earth stood quiet to hear.
Would God give up His Son?
But Son had prayed, and God had heard
The utterings of His prayer.
Then on the Cross Christ spoke His last,
And Father heard Him there.

And when in chapel, dimly lit,
We bow our heads to pray,
The Father, Son and Holy Ghost
Hear what we have to say.
Take care to pray,"Thy will be done
On earth through us today."
And pray for strength to do the task;
God hears His children pray!

# WHEN BROTHERS SANG

*A Confederate soldier told of troops singing carols across a battlefield and this thought: "I have seen the time when brothers were enemies. I pray for the time when I shall see enemies become brothers."*

Across a span men glared with ire
And blasted the other with cannon fire.
Musket and saber clashed by day.
At night the dead on the battlefield lay.
Twenty-four days in December had passed,
And darkness had fallen on the field at last,
And men fatigued, just stared at the sky,
And dreamed of a peace and began to cry.
Twenty-four days in December were gone,
And men, surrounded, lay all alone
And listened to the silence of battle zone
And spoke of memories of love and home.
No one knows who was the first who sang,
But across the deadly field there rang
Some words so dear to the human soul
They pierced with warmth the winter cold.
And some foe warmed by that wondrous heat
Returned the song in melody sweet,
And men who sang as one that song
Forgot their war, their hatred strong.
And were the angels out that night
They would have seen a wondrous sight
For all that field seemed lit up bright
By fire and song and Godly light.
As men to angels sang their hymn,
The angels must have looked at them
And wept a tear and smiled a smile
And stood in awe for that little while.
And one wrote late that night, "I see
When brothers behave like enemy."
And then he wrote, "To God I pray
To see enemies become brothers some day."

# TO A BUTTERFLY WITH A BROKEN WING

What can you say when a butterfly falls ne'er to fly again?
What words be found for a broken heart
that writhes in endless pain,
When life cannot return to one who's passed away,
And when  no prayer can give again to us our yesterday?

I watched him fall, that butterfly, that beauty from the sky.
And in the silence of the hour, I watched that beauty die.
Had he by awful twist of fate, instead been child or pet,
I'd have bound his limb and borne him on to doctor or to vet.

But butterflies do not heal well; they die from a broken wing.
So, what say you to a butterfly or friend you know is dying,
When pain you know will never cease, when love will ne'er return,
When hope is dashed upon a stone, when all you've built is ruined?

I'd say:
O, Butterfly, you brought to earth a beauty beyond the day
A grace upon the breeze, a joy along the way.
So, smile dear one, for all who've loved now sound the word,
You brought beauty to the world.

And I'd say,
O, Butterfly, you came my way and changed the way I see;
There's something now of you that now lives on in me.
So, smile again, and know as sure as heaven above is blue,
This world is better because of you.

And I'd say:
Can this be all, O Butterfly, you know far better than I,
You were born a worm, you were sealed to die,
You broke from the tomb as a beautiful butterfly,
Ah, yet awaits another birth beyond this earthly ring.

So, rest in peace my friend, earth's lovely one,
Beyond the dark there lies the rising sun.
You'll fly beyond the reach of earth upon eternal wings.
Just wait, dear one, and hear the angels sing.

# GOOD WILL SING THE VICTORY SONG

I have no thought to sit alone
And pine the day's demise,
Nor count the troubled hours that passed
Before the morning skies.
For God doth teach with each new dawn
That light subdues the night,
And good will sing the victory song
When dawns the morning light.

# LIFE'S REASON

So short a time upon this earth - We're born; we live; we die,
And ages pass upon the scene as winter birds fly by.
I sought a reason God gave life - Why born? Why live, then die?
Why struggle with the needs of earth  and see the starving cry?
Why must we yet endure the pains of aging bones and mind?
What is the reason we are here?  God, send to us a sign.

And then, I saw two, much in love, were walking hand in hand;
And saw a father teach his child to crawl and then to stand.
I saw a mother kiss a wound and heal it, then and there,
I saw a friend speak words of strength and touch the sufferer's hair.
And there amidst earth's greatest trials,
the storm, the quake, the flood,
I saw the winter's barren tree break forth in springtime bud.

And then I saw a given sign, revealed in nature's way:
An Oak, uprooted by the snow, in neighboring branches lay.
That tree was bent to breaking's point, but held with tender might
The one that fell with winter weight upon that winter night.
I thought how joyous it must be to have a neighboring friend
To catch us when our roots give way before the winter wind.

And then I thought how sweeter yet to be the neighboring arm
That holds our friend in fallen pain and keeps him safe from harm.
It seems we're placed upon this earth to grow, to learn, to love,
To share ourselves with those about, prepare for life above.
For living now within this age, we feel the token grace
Of greater love beyond our dreams that lives in heaven's face.

And yet we love not for that day but for the day at hand.
It seems that love makes sense of life. It must be God's own plan.

# LITTLE ACTS OF KINDNESS

Little drops of kindness flood my soul today
As sorrow, grief and pain are gently washed away.
And like a kindly rain, they soak beneath the skin
And cause an aching heart to leap with joy again.
And like the rain that soaks the newly planted seed
These little acts of kindness are exactly what I need.

From her bed she spoke, illness bound so long
Sunshine to the weak, example for the strong.
I wondered where she found the secret joy of life
That held her soul so tightly in victory and in strife.
I wondered how she found such joy amidst the pain.
Those little acts of kindness that gave her hope again.

She said there came another upon a cloudy day
Who spoke a word of kindness in a gentle way.
And like a gentle rain, it soaked her once again
Until she felt a hope take root so deep within.
She asked her friend where she had learned so deep a hope and joy
And she had said she learned it from the smile of her little boy.

# HISTORY IS FOR THE REWRITING

Like a hart that sprints from sight
And is soon lost in a thicket;
Like water falling from the edge of a glass
Onto the sand beneath it;
T'is time that flees and falls
So no hand can keep it.

We stare at the place where once it played.
Too soon its left our presence.
We long for time's untimely return,
Perpetual past existence.
Familiar grounds we've trod before
We seek with diligent persistence.

But time that's worn and passed away
We can't with prayer regain.
But, ah, the effects we can rewrite,
Relinquish ancient pain.
For history is yet within the writing
As once more we begin again.

# YOU ARE THE BLESSED RAIN

I think you are the drops of rain
That make the flowers grow,
That coarse their path through crevice depths
And make the rivers flow.

You are the patter on the pane
That cools the summer day,
Reminds me of the yesteryear
And friends along the way.

You fill the cisterns of my thought
And wash away the dust,
Refresh the air, replenish joy,
Restore my broken trust.

You are the blessed gift of rain
That God in grace doth send.
Your name is sent from heaven's hall,
That name we know as "Friend."

# THE GIFT OF RAIN

*Having read again the words, "The Lord causes it to rain upon the just and the unjust," I thought, "What a blessing." In that arid land the rains were life, and the very promise that sure blessings would fall upon all of us spelled hope.*

I walked in the eve of a summer day,
And felt the cooling rain soak my skin;
I shook a limb over the head of a friend
And watched his frown end;
I splashed through a puddle placed just for me
And felt a new spirit begin;
I raced through the field like a fleet-footed fawn
And felt like a child again.

The thunder and lightning flashed over my head,
And grass throbbed beneath my feet.
All about me were the wonders of life
Renewed by rain so sweet.
I believe that's the reason I love God so much:
He floods His blessings complete.
He pours them gently over my head
And freely covers my feet.

I do nothing of merit to earn His love,
But he sends it freely again.
So I walk in the eve of a summer day,
And feel the rains soak my skin,
And I think of the wondrous gifts of God,
And I pray: "Soak me, Lord, Again."

# DARKNESS

Touch me not, o morning light, for I am frail.
I fall beneath Thy might and creep away.
Yet, once in strength, I covered the land
And brought a chill to fainthearted souls.
My shadows set siege o'er city and hill
And reached into the hearts of those who wait.
For I am the night, and in my blackness, souls cried out.
I am the night, and where I live, fears may thrive,
Sounds intensify, and ghosts of the past, revive.
In my night all may hide but I,
For all may escape us but ourselves.
In the night we are captives and we are bound
By what we have seen and what we have been.
I am the night, and in me you see deeper into mind
And further into space than any other time
And both terrify.

I am the night, and in my reign the frightened
Think there will be no end,
And the hopeful know there will.
But as the nights before me, my time expires
And shows for all the world to see
That I am nothing but the absence of light
For I am darkness, and I am nothing.
And though I cry to Thee, o morning light,
"Touch me not," I have no defense.
And I creep away in the mist and song
You have brought to this, another day at dawn,
And my darkness is no more.

# A SONG UPON MY HEART

O, there's a song within my heart
That God has planted there,
That leads me through the darkness parts
And sings of His great care.

When birth of child swelled every vein
And joy filled every breast
He sang a song of sweet refrain -
the blessed and the best.

When sorrows poured like winter rain
His hand of love outstretched,
To sing me gently through the pain -
A lullaby of rest

I'll sing the song upon my heart
For all the joy He brings,
The love that God's own grace imparts
That made the angels sing.

# AGELESS JOY

There is a joy of youth that lasts
Within some grown folks' hearts -
A laughing face and playful soul
That joy to joy imparts.
Excitement is their daily friend,
Discovery their ally.
Though old in years, they're young at heart,
A twinkle in their eye.
Like them, I long to ever be
And keep the child inside,
For what's the use of living long
If joy does not abide.

# HERE'S A PURPOSE FOR THE NEW YEAR

So short a time upon this earth -
we're born; we live; we die,
And ages pass upon the scene
as winter birds fly by.
I sought a reason God gave life -
Why born? Why live, then die?
Why struggle with the needs of earth
and see the starving cry?
Why must we yet endure the pains
of aging bones and mind?
What is the reason we are here?
God, send to us a sign.
And then, I saw two, much in love,
Were walking hand in hand;
I saw a father teach his child
to crawl and then to stand.
I saw a mother kiss a wound
and heal it, then and there.
I saw a friend speak a word of strength
and touch the sufferer's hair.
And there amidst earth's greatest trials,
the storm, the quake, the flood,
I saw the winter's barren tree
break forth in springtime bud.
And then I saw a given sign,
revealed in nature's way:
An Oak, uprooted by the snow,
in neighboring branches lay.
That tree was bent to breaking's point,
but held with tender might
The one that fell with winter weight
upon that winter night.
I thought how joyous it must be

22

to have a neighboring friend
To catch us when our roots give way
before the winter wind.
And then I thought how sweeter, yet,
to be the neighboring arm
That holds our friend in fallen pain
and keeps him safe from  harm.

It seems we're placed upon this earth
to grow, to learn, to love,
To share ourselves with those about,
prepare for life above.
For living now within this age,
we feel the token grace
Of greater love beyond our dreams
that lives in heaven's face.
And yet we love not for that day
but for the day at hand.
It seems that love makes sense of life.
It must be God's own  plan.

# THE CHOICE

A bony, hairless tail, between his legs,
He crept across the open field nearby.
With shoulders hunched and canine head sunk low,
He caused an eerie form against the hazy sky.
The tiny, blackened birds still searched for seed
And hardly cast a glance upon his way.
And winter's harsh had thrown a piercing cold
Upon the heart of that winter day.
He slowly scratched amidst the trash that lay
Upon the frozen ground where folks had thrown,
And tried to burn, their garbage waste and such
In search of one unclaimed, forgotten bone.

I watched and feared that there in all his search
No food he'd find, no yet forgotten bone.
Then, in his weakened state he'd creep away
To sleep the everlasting sleep alone.
In quickened care, I made for him a plate
And bore that plate through winter's bitter chill
As close as dare I might approach his side
And left it there for him to eat at will.
With shaky legs he neared the plate I'd left
And sniffed the banquet food prepared for him.
He looked at me through sunset eyes, and then
He tucked his tail and crept into the dim.

Though day by day I set a plate for him
He never came and never dined upon the feast.
I never saw that bony dog again,
Nor yet can comprehend the man or beast
That stands by banquet plate where life resides
And turns aside to walk his life alone,
Who, in his fear, rejects the hope of hope
And in his hunger pains prefers a bone.

And Jesus sat upon the hill and wept
"Jerusalem, O would that you had known."
And men in pompous splendor made a choice:
Instead of kingdom feast they chose a bone.

# THERE'S A BEAUTY IN THE SUNSET

There's a beauty in the sunset over blackened hill
That cushions the red and feathery clouds above,
That holds the dying light within its hands
As though in tender, patient love.

An evening star keeps watch o'er all
As though the eye of God is set to shine
And guide the foot of traveling bands
Who seeking  hope, yet need a sign.

And beauty of the sunset still lives on in darkened hour
And echoes though the mind of those who might despair.
For though the darkness may command the night,
It dies at dawning's light and heaven's care.

Wondrous sunset beauty pales beneath the dawning light
As Sunrise sings a song of fresh redemptive birth
And souls arise and shake themselves alive again
And Father God reclaims the Mother Earth.

# CHALK CAN WRITE JUST WHAT IT'S TOLD

She stood before the class with chalk in hand
And said, "Within this small, white thing
Are many secrets not yet told."
And as we passed the chalk from hand to hand,
We fancied writing endless scrolls
Of all the secrets it might hold.
We wrote on board of truths and make believe
Till all we knew and all we'd heard
We wrote, then said, in pride, "Behold."
And yet, the chalk, or most of it, remained.
How may we from this chalk extrude
The secrets yet within its fold?
And though the mighty secrets of the land
Reside in silence deep inside,
The chalk can write just what it's told.
So how may we release these hidden truths
Lest we discover them anew
And learn by study, teacher, friend
The lessons that our life doth hold.

# A FINAL NOTE

He sat in a chair, slumped and still.
A note beside him fell.
They say he shot himself at noon
And wrote the note to tell
The desperate way he looked at life
And sorrows he had known.
T'was found that way by evening light,
So sadly there alone,
A friend of mine - just learned to drive -
- A child of sixteen years.
I wept that night a sorrowing tear
To hear his wanton fears.
Within the note he told his pain,
The struggles of his mind,
The classmates who in thoughtless ways
Had been to him unkind,
The jokes they pulled, the tales they told
In unsuspecting ways.
And though he told of family hurts,
The loneliest of days
Were made by those who could have seen
His yearning to be "in,"
And should have loved and helped him know
And could have been his friend.
At service time the room was filled
With youth on every pew,
A sight he would have not believed,
An honor he was due.
We talked of funny, happy times,
The words we wish we'd said
That might have eased his silent pain
Or stilled his daily dread.
And though too late for one of us,
We all resolved to say
The words of friendship that we feel
To others every day.

# YE WARRIORS OF THE WAY

All ye warriors of the Way,
Hold your weapons high
Await the breaking of the day
And the captain's cry.

No iron and steel your weapons made,
No bombs and tanks pursue.
No army hosts nor strong brigade
Parade in battle view.

Your weapons are but tiny things
Or so the world declares.
They are the gifts the Savior brings,
The blessings that He shares.

The love, the faith, the hope He give,
The strength within His plan,
The times He stirs, remolds, forgives,
The times He holds our hand.

And yet these tiny things endure
Beyond our ups and downs
Until we stand with hope secure
And wear the victor's crown.

# I GIVE MY LIFE FOR YOU

He watched his birth and heard him cry
And thought, "What will I do?"
And time and time it seemed to him,
The days too swiftly flew.
He saw him crawl and walk and talk,
And said,
"I'd give my life for you."

He stood at the bed, the side of his child
And thought,"What can I do?"
He watched the pain those final days,
The illness through and through.
And helpless as it seemed to him,
He said,
"I'd give my life for you."

And on a hill Another knelt
And thought, "What must I do?"
Another time, another place,
He prayed for strength anew.
And Son of Man raised to His feet,
And said,
"I'll give my life for you."

And on a Hill not far away
They thought, "What does He do?
He freely gives His life for us
A second chance, t'is true."
And humbly kneeling at His feet,
We pray,
"I give my life to You."

For God so loved the world that He gave His
only begotten Son, and we find
there is only one true gift we can give in return:
OURSELVES!

# A VIEW OF A HUNGRY WORLD

*With caring or calloused eye we watch and hear*
*the needs of the world, and so I submit...*

See the hungry people roam
Cross the deserts far from home.
Barren limb and hollow eyed,
Thousands daily die.
Mother with an empty breast
Holds her baby to her chest
And doesn't know the quiet child
Does quietly die.

Father in his skin and bone
Scratches in the dirt alone,
Searches in the scorching sun
With eyes to dry to cry.
And son stares out in empty glare
Swollen belly, falling hair,
And hardly feels the pesty stings
On eyes too dry to cry.

We turn our heads so not to see
These homeless horde on our TV,
Pretend they do not still exist,
Pretend they do not die.
For we have much upon our plate
And we must not dare be late
To our club or party night.
And we forget them by and by.

... or ...

The anguish of their painful plight,
Their hunger and their frightened flight,

Pain our souls and pierce our hearts.
And call the caring soul to pray.
And from our plenty, bountiful store
A gift of love we pull once more
And pray some pain we may relieve
And save some life today.

# AROUND THE BEND

My spirit roamed through slum-med street
In search of hope amidst despair
And found among the wretchedness
The voice of God was nestled there.
I met a man of twisted limb
Of ragged clothes without a place
To safely rest his head at night
And yet he wore a smiling face.
I asked of him his secret strength
And this he told that night to me:
"There're men who live upon this street
In sorrow, filth and agony.
Their world extends to yonder bend -
No further see, no further go;
And so they live, condemned to die,
Imprisoned in the life they know.
But me, I see beyond the bend
A place where filth is washed away,
Where those I've loved in life still live,
Where darkness turns to glorious day.
Beyond the bend I see Him wait
His hand in love reached out to me.
And I shall smile though ragged, poor
So long as Him I see."
And I arose to go my way
And ambled on toward yonder bend.
A smile now crept across my face.
Around the bend awaits my friend.

*I wonder what would happen were we to speak the words of encouragement we offer our families to the whole world.*

# THE NOTE

A love so dear I had to write a note to say t`was true
That in this life, the greatest joy is saying, I love you.
And having writ, I closed my eyes to think how I could say,
That you in wonder, beauty pose the sunlight of my day.
A little gust of wind, so light, like infant breath it blew,
Caressed my note by phantom hands and stole my note to you.

It bore the sheet with three small words across the village town,
And there before a weeping lass it gently laid it down.
Her broken heart; her love confused, her
soul was pained and bruised.
She saw the note and read the words where written, "I love you."
"It is a sign from heav'n," she spoke, "For someone loves me yet."
A trace, a line, perhaps a smile, a joy she can't forget.

The little breath of breeze blew on, the note upon its wing
And traveled to a far-off town where mourners tried to sing.
There sorrow gripped the aching heart. An only child had died.
And as a butterfly in flight with no where else to hide,
The note fell there before the crowd as if from heaven's blue.
"Behold," one said as yet he read, "God writes this:`I Love you.'"

Then having read the note to all, he tossed it in the air,
And then, the wondrous breath of life, carried it off from there.
The words I wrote to you, my love, are words the world doth need.
So let the note be on its way for all the world to read.
So let me write, nay, speak the words I wrote to you that day
And find a way to all the world these needed words to say.

# GIANTS WALK THE EARTH

O, once great giants walked the earth,
And valor ruled the heart,
And dreams and honor were life's worth,
And faith it's greatest part.
There was a time when Right was Might
And Cause led hearts to sing,
A time when in the darkest night
The call to arms would ring,
And giants laid down their selfish toil
To join the urgent bell
And marched away to foreign soil
Where many giants fell.
And though their frames beneath the sod
Lie marked or lost to man,
Their souls are known to a loving God
Who holds them in His hand.
In human hearts their spirits pray
To plant heroic song,
Give cause to Giants of today
And reason to be strong.
And so amidst the earthly pain,
Amidst the human strife,
The Giants walk the earth again
The heroes of this life.

# AN ANCIENT MAN

He sat relaxed beside the fire,
And smoke encircled his head.
A woven cloth embraced his lap,
And hardly a word he said.

He could not stand upon his feet
Or grasp a loving hand.
He could not see to call a name.
He was an ancient man.

He gazed into the flickering flame
And dreamed of years gone by
And sometimes told of a golden age -
A laugh, a smile, a cry.

Once, he ran with fawn-like gait
And spoke with golden tongue,
But that was long, so long ago,
When strength and life were young.

I sat with him beside the fire
And smelled the bitter smoke
And longed to see the loved one past,
Of whom He often spoke.

He said one night t'was time to go
And join his lovely bride.
He laid his pipe beside his chair
And closed his eyes and died.

And now I sit beside the fire
And dream of days gone by.
I see him in the flickering flame
And hear his faintest sigh.

I speak to him when all is still
And thank him for the joy
He bred in me, he showed to me
When I was but a boy.

I hope in heaven's hilltop home
God has a roaring flame,
And winter finds him sitting there
When someone calls his name

And as he turns to face the call,
He sees his lovely bride.
He hardly speaks a single word;
His smile he cannot hide.

The "king of silence" he's been called,
Extends his crippled hand
And holds his joy of life again
And finds the strength to stand.

And if through all eternity,
With loved one by His side,
He lives the joy he gave to earth,
He never really died.

# THE CROSS OF GLASS

There hangs a Cross upon my pane,
And when I open up the shade,
Through this Cross of Glass
I see the world that God has made.

And when at first I hung it there,
I saw the Cross, and gazed upon it.
Yet, now when at the world I look,
There hangs the Cross, and I look through it.

# TREEHOUSE OF DREAMS

The old tree stood with naked bough beside the garden wall.
The golden leaves caressed its roots.  I saw the last one fall.
When but a child, I loved to sit upon the old tire swing
And feel the breeze upon my face and hear the Robin sing.
And wedged between two mighty boughs, high up above the ground,
A tree house built of weathered boards with nails and cable bound,
A rope of knots, our only stair, a trap, our only door.
We sat secluded in our room upon a boarded floor.

And secrets flowed like summer rain, and
dreams sometimes were born
High up above the worldly pains and safe from hapless scorn.
And we could dream whatever dream  the Master Dreamer made,
Pursue whatever hope He gave, whatever path He laid.
But those were years far in the past, forgotten far too long,
And dreams have fallen, like the leaves and like the silenced song,
Encumbered by the weight of pain, entrapped by earthly snare
And left in ample disarray in the tree house way up there.

They came with saw and axes sharp to hew the great oak down,
And so I climbed the ancient stair far up above the ground,
And as a man sat once again upon the boarded floor
And prayed aloud: "O Master of the dream,
those ancient dreams restore.
Help me once more to be a child, adventuresome and bold.
Help me pursue the dreams I've seen, the dreams my memories hold.
And though my body through the years has aged, and always will,
May dreams stay young and hopeful yet and keep me dreaming still."

I watched the tree, its mighty fall, its crash upon the ground
And saw the house that we had loved explode with deafening sound.
And all its secret dreams blew free and floated through the air.
So, if you dream a childhood dream and wonder whence and where,
Perhaps, it blew on summer breeze from an ancient childhood day

(For dreams don't die; they simply fade and slowly slip away)
To find another childlike mind, as if on angels' wing
Where dreamers live, and fancies fly, and hopes and hearts yet sing.

# THE SWIMMING HOLE

In the Swimming hole as boys we played
And splashed and swam from shore to shore
And smoked the grapevine pipes we made
And swore to be friends forevermore.
To strip and dive and duck and splash -
No grief allowed within that place -
To skip a stone and belly-crash.
I now recall their every face.

I stand beside that ancient hole,
Its silent waters seem to long
To hear the laughing sounds of old
As robins wait the morning song.
The faces I had learned so well
And swore as friend to n'er forget
Have scattered more than I can tell
But not forgot, nor e'er forget.

I peered into the swimming hole
As if beneath its watered dark
Might lie some mystery yet untold,
Some flame to reignite a spark.
And as I peered, I dropped a tear
That fell upon my imaged face,
And waters danced with ghoulish cheer
And spread my face o'er all the place.

I bowed to pray by evening light,
"God bless my friends where e'er they are,
And like the ripples in the night
Please send my prayer both near and far,
And touch them now with peace and grace;
And in Thy mercy, hold them near,
And may  life's pressure n'er erase
The memories of the friends  held dear."

# I'VE WANDERED THE FOREST CALLED FEAR

I've wandered the forest called "Fear,"
And seen behind each lurking tree
That monstrous form that hides and waits
To jump and frighten me.

I've plod the desert dunes, "Despair,"
And seen the unending sand
Where hope is parched 'neath noonday sun,
Where arid hopes can't stand.

I've sat alone in the Garden, "Grief,"
Where silent flowers bloom,
And memory tears an aching heart
In darkened, evening gloom.

I've shot the river we call "Rage,"
And felt its torrent force
That swept my weakened soul away
Upon its mindless course.

And all along these pit-filled ways,
By day or darkened night,
There moved a power of present strength
Of endless, saving might.

No fear or grief, despair or rage
Could keep Him long away
For in His love He held my hand,
Redeeming every day.

From desert sands to unused tomb
He'd walked the painsome way,
And now He's come to lead me through
Because of Easter Day.

# GOD'S IN A MOMENT LIKE THAT

A tender blade of grass this spring
Has cut through an asphalt way.
Surely God's in strength like that.

A gentle ewe has stood her ground
And saved her lamb today.
Surely God's in courage like that.

A pretty bird has laid her eggs
Outside my door last night.
Surely, God's in trust like that.

And all the world stands still to hear
Her song at morning light.
Surely, God's in sounds like that.

Butterflies return to where t'were born
To faithfully give birth.
Surely God's in resolve like that.

And rains fall down and rivers flow,
And the sun doth warm the earth.
Surely God's in grace like that.

And I in gladness bow my head
And shed a joyous tear.
The God in heaven's eternity
I know is also near.
And, Lo, God's in a moment like that.

# THE FEEDING

He fed the crowd on mountaintop
A few small loaves and fish,
And yet their hearts were filled that day
With more than they could wish.
Those who longed for love were loved;
The hopeless filled with hope;
The lost were found by friends and kin
Along that mountain slope.
He fed the griever a meal of joy;
The lonely met a friend;
The sad attracted by His word
Felt happy once again.
The sick forgot their sickened state;
Infirmities were healed
As Jesus fed the multitude
Upon that eastern hill.
T'was not the fish or yet the loaves
That held the power that day.
T'was Jesus feeding those who came
And walked along His way.
T'was those who opened wide the door,
The hungry, lost and least,
That  saw the Bread of Heaven speak
And fed upon His feast.

# THE VICTOR'S TEAR

*A soldier, after a difficult battle in which many were killed - friend and*
*foe, sat and wept, not for those who fell but for those who loved them.*
*Those who died, died for a cause in which they believed. ...but those*
*who remained! Their universe stood still, for each one who died was the*
*cause for living for someone who loved them. And the mighty soldier*
*said, "I vowed to celebrate victory tomorrow. Tonight, I will weep."*

Across the world a battle stirs and human flesh is cheap
And children die for freedom's sake, and mothers, hidden, weep.
Across the world the children starve and wander empty streets
While banquets spread cross other lands,
they search for scraps to eat.
And millions walk a parch-ed land without a place to sleep
And lie beneath a withered bough, for human flesh is cheap.
And women hide behind a veil and fear to show their face,
And freedom is forgotten dream in that embattled place
And lest we think that flesh is cheap when unnamed children die,
And families walk the pain-filled trail beneath the cloudless sky,.
And lest we think that life goes on when unknown loved ones die,
May we, within a broken heart, hear Jesus softly cry.
The least of these upon this earth are great within His light,
And human flesh is far from cheap in God's eternal sight.
And every time a child of His doth die by want or pain
He weeps again in agony - a part of Him is slain.
Someone's own universe stands still, each time a loved one dies,
The great and small and in between, a friend or foe, He cries.
When freedom is the victor's chant, and hope parading, smiles
Look deep into the pain-filled eyes of those who lost a child.
And victory, though great, indeed, and worthy sacred price
Is muted by its cost and claim of human sacrifice.
And worthy soldiers kneel beside their beds before they sleep
And weep a tear for those who died, for human flesh is not cheap.
And through the distance, God to man, an awesome sound is heard
As falling tears unite the hearts of victors and the Word.
And may our prayer for peace abide upon this fragile earth -
The sacred price for human life, our Savior's holy birth.

# AS EVENING FALLS

When evening falls and sun doth set
And darkness claims the sky,
One Light remains in perfect place
To set our compass by.
It's guided ships o'er ocean wave
Across the salty foam,
A constant light in darkest hour,
And led the traveler  home.

And in a world by trouble strained,
I search the darkened blue.
When all nailed down is coming loose,
I seek a light as true.
I quested long o'er land and sea
And traveled twisted trail,
And tested power, wealth and clan,
And saw them dim and fail.

And then I found the One who seeks.
He found my searching soul,
A frightened lamb in darkness lost,
Brought safely to the fold.
A Shepherd, Friend, Eternal Bread,
Example as I roam,
A constant Light in darkest hour.
To lead me safely home.

# BENEATH THE BOUGHS

I lay beneath the Springtime tree
And breathed the springtime air
And saw the heavens, speckled green
And knew that God was there.

I lay beneath the summer tree
A shelter o'er my bed,.
And thanked my God for keeping me -
Protection o'er my head.

I lay beneath the autumn bough
With leaves of every hue.
Its beauty moved my very soul
To loving thoughts of you.

I lay beneath the winter form,
A wondrous, lovely sight
For God replaced the fallen leaves
With stars that very night.

# I'M GLAD

I thank my Lord that I can see
The wondrous things of Earth.
I know the Hands that made it all
Give hope and life and birth.

I'm glad that in this life we have
That beauty outlives shame,
And hope is more than blind denial
And someone knows my name.

I'm glad that flowers bloom all year
Throughout the summer heart
And poke their heads through fallen snow,
Through winter's evening sleet.

I'm glad that memories of pain
Pass on and fade a way,
But goodness lives forever on
To bless another day.

I'm glad that though it sometimes seems
That evil ways will win,
That goodness, love and Godly ways
Stand victors in the end

I'm glad that when I suffer tears
It's not a lonely pain,
But outstretched hands of loving friends
Are offered me again.

I'm glad, I guess, above all else
This world so wondrous stands
Not by the puny mind of man
But in God's loving hands.

# LOOKING THROUGH

O, in a world that's sorrow prone
There're people who rejoice,
And midst their tears and agony
Sing out with joyful voice.

And in a world of solitude
They sing great songs of praise,
And seem to hear a harmony,
Angelic chorus raise.

And pain is but a fleeting thing.
They look beyond its power,
And know that heaven's for eternity,
And pain's but for an hour.

And when they fall, they stand again
And trust their call once more,
As eagles seem inclined to fly,
They spread their wings and soar.

I pray that I shall have a heart
That looks beyond the pain
And knows that summer flowers bloom
Because of April rain.

And as I wait I pray to sing
The self-same songs of praise,
And feel the joy of company
When songs of hope I raise.

# THE GREATEST GIFT OF ALL

*Above all, I remember the time we spent together, my father and I. So, I share these lines with you.*

He gave his child a cherished gift
One early day in Spring.
I held the gift within my hand,
A long awaited thing.
I thought that gift would surely last,
That gift within my hand,
And I would play each day with it.
I lost it in the sand.
And many Springs have come and gone;
The gift I don't recall.
I can't begin to see its shape.
I don't remember it at all.

He gave an hour to his child.
He thought a simple thing,
But somewhere deep within my heart
A voice began to sing.
Its words I have not yet forgot;
Can't lose them in the sand.
They go with me where'er I go
And bless this weary man.
I pray that as I age with years,
This secret I recall:
The time you give with your own child's
The greatest gift of all.

# A PRAYER TO THE PRINCE OF PEACE

## THE PAIN
O, Little town of Bethlehem, thy streets are racked with pain
Where mortar blasts destroy the past and mortal men are slain
We hear the roaring cannon, the mothers' awful wail
O, come again, O Prince of Peace, our Lord, Emmanuel.

## THE CRY
And in their dark, the children sit and long for light of day.
And in the still the mothers cry, and this is what they say:
O, set a light before our eyes that we may surely see
And sound Your love across the skies, O God, eternally.
And on the heaven's window seal, God placed a candle bright
To call the seeker home again, through darkest, lonely night.

## THE GIFT
And far beyond the star that shone on Christmas long ago
The loving God from heaven's seat looks on the earth below,
And once again the carolers sing the songs we've grown to love,
And once again the hopeful pray and seek the light above.
But lo, the light that lit the sky and made the shepherds shout
Has come to earth on trees and things.  It's shining all about.
The Prince of Peace from heaven's halls, by wondrous, holy birth
Has seen the needs across these lands and come to dwell on earth.

## THE RESPONSE
What does the Lord require of me that peace may come again?
That haunting cry of mother's grief that holds her infant slain?
O, God, Who gives me life and breath; oh, what have I to dare
But this poor soul, this single voice?  What more have I to share?
I lay myself before the King; 'tis all that I can do.
He smiles and says, "That's all I ask.  The greatest gift is you!

# AND THE PEOPLE CRIED

And the people cried!

Protruding bellies, bony ribs,
Opened eyes, hungry flies,
Mother starved; baby died;
And all the people cried.

Divided earth, fallen stone,
Earthquake shake, polluted lake,
Home collapse, ten-thousands died;
And all the people cried.

Beaten land at civil war,
Brothers fight, human plight;
Mothers prayed; their children died,
And all the people cried.

Twisted steel, two fallen giants.
Terror strikes, but courage lives.
Thousands fell though heroes tried,
And all the people cried.

And in the midst, a voice is heard,
"Why hast Thou forsaken me,
And tossed my richest dream aside?"
And all the people cried.

And in the sorrow there is heard
"My Son, too, by sin was slain,
And on the Cross was crucified
And all the heavens cried.

"But this, please know beyond a doubt,
Though grief and pain abide,

I was with you as you cried."
And all the tears were dried..

If God be for us, WHO can be against us?

# FRIEND

And this I've found upon the earth:
That Friends make life worth living,
And lest we lose this fondest part,
It's love we best be giving.
If I could be whate'er I want,
I'd choose to be a friend.
Engrave upon my granite stone
When life on earth doth end,
And make the letters bold and clear,
These words:  "He was our friend."

# BY MY BED AT NIGHT

"My God"
He sits beside my bed at night
To watch me soundly sleep.
His face aglow; his hands at work
To silent vigil keep.
The last I see before I sleep,
The first by morning light.
And when the day has been its worst
He's with me through the night.
And when I'm up and all about
I see him everywhere.
He sings the mighty Mickey song,
Is heard on courthouse square.
He travels with me every place;
I seek his friendly face.
In him I trust and must depend
Upon the call he sends.
He is my friend, my steady rock,
He is my watch, my clock.

# THE SWING

*Hanging by old, rusty chains in an ancient vine-covered arbor, the weatherbeaten swing beckoned in the gentle breeze as if inviting the weary to rest. I often accepted, choosing to sit quietly in the cool haven and watch, simply watch. The swing moved so slightly as if propelled by a secret and mighty hand. The world before me seemed to sway in a rhythm similar to a heartbeat, the heartbeat of creation. My worries melted and ran through my fingers;. I could not hold them. And peace, like a whisper, cradled my soul. And somehow in those moments, I saw God.*

In the quiet of a summer day when sun creatures run to hide,
And morning blooming Glories tuck themselves inside -
When shadows disappear beneath the traveler's feet,
And only desert things enjoy the noonday heat,
I sit awhile to contemplate the mystic songs of earth
And sing the words of joyous life amidst creation's birth.
The old and weatherbeaten swing beneath the sheltering green
Looks out upon a wood of ferns, a cool, delightful scene.
And while arrays of tiny things play in the wooded shade,
I think about the Lord at hand and all the things He's made.
There gently flits a butterfly upon his graceful wings.
A beetle clicks; a frog gives heart, mysterious, wondrous things.
There blows a cool and gentle breeze across my moistened face,
And bears with it the jasmine scent, a gift of heaven's grace.
And as the skies grow still and dim, the heavenly choirs come out,
And voices sing from trees and shrubs; God's chorus all about!
Before mankind did walk this earth, the creatures sang their song,
The flowers bloomed, the breezes blew, the trees grew tall and strong.
And now I hear His chorus sing, unto this grateful ear.
This garden place God made for us, I feel His presence here.

# FORGIVEN

Excuses melt and roll away
For while they stand within the day,
At night they're weak and bare.
They stand by bed and stare
Until disclaimed, then melt away.

And guilt, that plundering hun,
Sets siege on soul and sun,
And by its siege beclouds the day.
In dreariness, won't go away
For all the sorrow that it's done.

Escape, the dream of captured men
From all the dungeons they're in,
Eludes the soul, outruns the mind.
The freshest path's most hard to find,
And's heard: "You made the mess you're in."

So blot it out!  Remove it, bare,
And do the deed that will declare
That puny past or shameful sin
Is not the shape your future's in,
But hope survives the deadly dare.

For who has not, within this day,
Behaved in some regretful way?
If all who fall must stay aground,
Where may the upright then be found
'Til mercy melts the guilt away?

# VICTORY'S IN THE BATTLE

I had a dream of victory
To win a battle true,
And out across the scorching sand
I raced, my work to do.
And soon a celebrated cry
Was heard across the land
For I had won my battle well
And raised the victor's hand.
But victory can easily bring
Defeat upon the heart.
If that is all the dreamer dreamed
It leaves no power to start
For victory has an ending sound
Of work accomplished, done
That locks the victor in the past
With laurels he has won.
It was the dream that led him on
To war against the wrong.
It was the journey's treacherous trail
That called and made him strong.
Let those who win a victory
Beneath God's brilliant sun
Arise again with sword in hand
With other battles to be won.
For 'tis the dream, the journey's call,
That led him bravely on,
For from the dream that he is giv'n
The conquering soul is born.

Without a dream, a people perish

# THE MAGI

*New life began for the Wisemen who knelt before*
*the infant Jesus.  On Epiphany we*
*celebrate  their discovery, and for those who celebrate,*
*this, indeed, becomes a new year.*

As fresh as infant's breath, as clean
As freshly fallen snow,
A year is born upon the earth
As wintry winds still blow,
As peas and jowl and Auld Lang Syng
Greet infant fair with glee,
For all the hope it brings to earth,
For all the energy.
And plodding yet across the sands
Come wisemen from afar.
To greet a child yet born a king,
They need a heavenly star.
Still, at the infant year they find
An infant hope is born,
And gold and myrrh and frankincense
They lay before His throne.
And infant born in stable den
Would shine with brighter light
And greet the birth of countless years
As on that fateful night.
So, we with wisemen from of old,
Still come to manger rare
And know that at this bright new year
Eternal hope we share.
Yet, more than birth of but a year
That fades with evening sun,
Eternity has come to earth
And hope to everyone.

# THE SHEPHERD LAD

*Ever thought what it may have been like for the shepherds?*

The shepherd lad just sat with men and watched the sheep by night.
"I wonder what the singing means and why the sky's so bright?"
He'd often heard his mother say that God would come to earth;
That here, some day in Bethlehem, would be the wondrous birth.

But to a child who's never seen, or even thought to see,
How could he know what God had done or yet would bring to be?
"I guess I'll follow all my friends and have a little fun;
I'll play and laugh and share a tale when all is said and done."

So off he went with shepherds few, as angels warmed the sky,
And came with them to Bethlehem and stable warm and dry.
A baby lay there just inside all wrapped in swaddling clothes,
A mother, father, shepherds, too, all knelt in prayerful pose.

Our laddie stopped at stable door and tried in vain to see,
And bowed his head and crept inside as quietly as could be.
He made his way to manger side and held his staff in hand.
He looked into the manger bed and saw the Son of Man.

The shepherd lad just sat and thought of all that he had seen -
More beautiful than is the spring when fields are freshly green.
Though time has passed and ages gone since in the stable dim,
The shepherd knows that what he saw has touched and altered him.

For once you hear the angels sing and see your sky all lit,
And once you make your way to Him, you know what it all meant:
He is the Son of God most sure and brings a peace to earth,
And angels sing, but souls do, too, at such a wondrous birth.

So close...so close!

# THE INN KEEPER

"I fail to see what I can do,"
The wearied keep said,
"To find within this crowded inn
E'en one yet empty bed."
And then he turned to walk away
But stopped and quietly said,
"There is a spot that's warm at night
Where animals are fed -
A stable den behind this inn
Where you may spend the night
And rest your souls on manger straw
Until the morning light."
And while the keeper kept his post,
The couple made their way
To find the creature den
And there await the day.
And as the hour waned away,
The keeper closed his book,
And as he passed the stable door,
He paused to take a look.
The stable where he sent the two
Seemed strangely lit that night,
And shepherds knelt about the stall;
A star above gave light.
The keeper thought an angel's wing
He saw within the den
And paused to ask of stable hands
What wonders they had seen.
"Oh, 'tis a child, and just a child
That's born upon the hay,
And 'tis the shepherds from the field
Who've gathered here to pray."
He took a step within the den,
But stopped. 'Twas heard to say,

"'Tis just a child, and I am tired."
He turned and went away.
And as he walked toward home and bed
He saw the heavenly light,
But never knew, o, just how close
To heav'n he'd come that night.

# WHO IS THIS CHILD?

Who is this child in manger straw,
And warmed by rags and things?
And what this sound I vaguely hear,
That sounds like angel wings?
And what's his name, this infant here,
Where Shepherds kneel and pray,
And wisemen offer gifts to him,
And kneel in stable hay?
I heard someone just speak his name.
T'was "Jesus", I heard him say,
For God would save the searching soul,
The Life, the Truth, the Way!
And how could one child do the good
I heard them testify?
And how could he upon this hay
Heal broken hearts that cry?
A Roman soldier came to see
What led to all the fuss.
He filled the doorway with his size,
And spoke to each of us.
"What goes on here?" He said aloud,
His arms across the door.
He blocked the warming morning sun.
His shadow marked the floor.
It formed a fearsome Roman cross
That marked the manger bed
And seemed, at least, to all of us
To mark the baby's head.
I smiled a smile that wondrous day.
A child was born, you see,
And I could love that child with all my heart
And He would so love me.
And though I smiled a smile that day,
A tear ran down my eye,

For loving Jesus, full of grace,
Upon the cross would die.
How could I know the wondrous truth
That all the world would sing.
Though infant born was crucified:
Nobody kills the King!

# JOSEPH

There was a man whose faith was tried
In Nazareth town one night.
An angel of the Lord came down
In majestic light
Who said that Mary, his betrothed,
Would bear the Son of God.
A mighty Counselor, Royal Priest,
Messiah, Jessie's rod.
"How can this be?" this Joseph cried.
"She's known not yet a man.
To take her now to be my bride,
I know not if I can."
"The Holy Spirit's come to her,
And she shall bear His child."
The angel left, then, in a flash,
For Joseph to decide.
And Joseph rose at breaking dawn
And took his love to wed
For he had trusted in his heart
The words the angels said.
He led her safe to Bethlehem
And found a stall for sleep,
He knelt beside her through the night -
His promises to keep.
And there amidst the animals
And warmed by manger hay,
The child of God was born that night,
And it was Christmas Day.
Of all the people kneeling there,
By Joseph I'm most awed.
For he in selfless thoughtfulness
Took up the task of God
To raise this child Whom God had sent
In God's selected way -

To teach, to serve, to heal, to die
On Calvary someday.
And Joseph, in his humble trust,
He did it all for love
For Mary whom he so adored
And for his God above.
And so we thank this God who sent
His son upon the hay
That men like Joseph kneeling there
Are part of Christmas day.

# WHY IS THE EARTH SO BRIGHT?

A star looked down from heaven's height
And saw the Earth aglow with light.
For Christmas Eve had come again
That cold and frosty winter night.

"Why this?" he asked. "Why's earth so bright?
What deed of grace doth so delight?
What beauty leads the human heart
To make the earth such an awesome sight?"

And Wondrous Star that shown so bright
Upon the ancient Christmas night
Spoke out and said, "A child was born
On manger straw by candle light.

"And holy angels took their flight
And winged their way to earth that night.
Believing shepherds left their flock
To see the strange and wondrous sight.

"Believers yet with great delight
Still set their world aglow tonight.
The Son of God has come to earth -
This Jesus Christ, Eternal Light.".

# CONVERSATION WITH A STAR

Little star, shining bright,
Tell me of the night.
Tell me how the angels sang.
Tell me of that night.
High above the shepherds' field shone a mystic light,
And deep into their yearning hearts set their souls afright
Even as the angels sang at this awesome sight.
Little star, shining bright,
Tell me more of this.
Tell me how they found the child
On this night of bliss
Up they rose from Shepherds' fire; Walked through evening mist;
Came to stand at stable door where earth and heaven kissed,
And knelt before the manger stall on a night like this.
Little star, shining bright,
Tell me even more.
Tell me what the shepherds did
Upon that far off shore.
They knelt with empty hands, yet, hands that richly bore
The gift of life and love and even so much more,
And pledged, this Child to love and ever to adore.
Little star, shining bright,
What wonder must have been.
Tell me what the shepherds did
When they left that den.
To shepherd care they went their way to do their work again,
But ne`er were they quite the same as they had early been
For God had touched their very souls and made them pure within.
Little star, shining bright
With Thine eyes that see,
Tell me what the shepherds saw
And what it means to me.
The shepherds saw the Son of God sent down for them and thee.
They saw the hope of life and love God sends eternally.

They saw what God doth pray, on Christmas all may see.

And the star blazed in the heavens and the angels sang!
And it was Christmas!

# IN A MANGER BED

In a manger made a bed,
Lay a baby, Angels said.
Shepherds heard the angels sing,
"In the manger lies a king."
From the field by a star's great light
They made their way that fateful night
And found the babe in swaddling clothes
And knelt in silent, prayerful pose.
How tiny, small, this infant king,
About whose birth the heavens sing!
They wondered how this tiny child
So innocent, meek and mild
Could be the One the prophets said,
So tiny lay he in his bed.
And yet today, though years have flown
This infant o'er the world is known
As Savior, Lord, Messiah, King.
The faithful still with caroles sing,
For t'was the night of wondrous birth
When angels winged their way to earth,
When Father, God from heaven's store
Sent His Son for evermore.
And when the sun fades yonder way
Beyond the hills at close of day,
And Christmas Eve is here again,
As fresh a sound as desert rain,
And peace is felt in every heart
We hear the heavenly voices start,
And once again in manger den
An infant King is born again.

# THE HEM OF HIS GARMENT

He walked the street with dignity,
Disciples at His side -
The poor, the weak, the lame the blind,
The children none could hide.
They pressed His way at every turn,
Called out His name aloud,
This motley, eager, hungry band,
This hopeful, prayerful crowd.
And I, behind this mass of folk
And weak by sickened pain,
Determined yet to touch His hand
And be made whole again -
If not the hand, then just the robe.
I pushed.  The crowd gave way.
Behold, I fell upon the street.
Before His feet I lay.
He paused, and with my shaking hand
I touched His garment hem,
And saw Him stop.  A power passed,
A grace to me from Him.
For in the days that were to pass
By faith and prayer I found
The secret of His wondrous love
While prostrate on the ground:
That He had sought me all the while
That I was seeking Him,
And He had led me through the crowd
To touch His garment's hem.

# PALM SUNDAY THOUGHTS

## ... OF ONE

He rode in pomp and power
And entered on steed of fire,
A king and victor proud
As trumpets blasted loud,
And men reduced to dust
Before this king of lust.
So where, his strength and might?
Vanished in forgotten night!

## ... OF ANOTHER

He came on humble ass
Without the trumpet blast,
But met by palm and shout,
A king, without a doubt.
The King of Peace, He came,
And Jesus was His name.
And where's this King, I pray?
With us, alive, today!

The lonely, in their prayer,
Discover he is there.
The lost who seek their way
Meet Him at dawning's day.
The wretched, torn by strife,
Are given peaceful life.
And all who seek His face
Shall find eternal grace.
For love is stronger yet than might
And lightens e'en the blackest night;
And good outlasts the greatest wrong
And sings for hope the final song;
And weapons melt to ore and clay
While good lives on another day.

# THEY MAY HAVE LAUGHED

They may have laughed, that rugged throng, at Him,
When they saw Jesus ride into Jerusalem.
They may have shouted songs and clapped their hands
As Jesus walked with motley band.
And when He chased the sellers from their temple posts
They may have cheered the most.
They may have chanted as most mobs would
When Jesus by Barabbas stood.
They may have jeered at every moan
Of Jesus along the streets of cobblestone,
As He bore the  Cross of Light
Toward waiting Golgatha's height,
And when they nailed Him to the Cross
And words of anger were all but lost,
They may have cadence kept,
While kneeling mother wept.
But when He died, no shout was heard,
But yet a whisper, yet a word:
"Surely," one at watch was heard to cry,
This is the Son of God, I testify."

# THOUGHTS OF A CENTURION

I've seen them die on the cross before
These wretched slaves of Roman rule.
Yea, in my youth by Caesar's might,
Thousands lined this Judaen Street,
And yet today as three are nailed
The waters churn at Bethsaida's Pool.
A strangeness lights Jerusalem's sky:
And darkness stalks Jerusalem's heat.

The nails I drove are straight and clean
So, let him frail and shout and weep,
He cannot touch and change or threaten now,
He cannot reach me from His Cross.
And yet, I watch with holden breath
And feel in me, my spirit leap
For from the Cross He touched my soul
And found the heart I thought was lost.

Upon that Cross was more than man.
Beneath that Cross was more than guilt.
"Forgive them, Father," He had said.
"This is God's Son," I had replied.
And e'en today the Cross remains
A symbol of the faith He built
And of the Life He brought to us
The day that Love was **Crucified.**

# BLACK SATURDAY

The darkest day the world has known,
The day He lay entombed -
No hope, no life, no promise shown -
And faith severely doomed.
He could have called a legion down,
Protect Him from the Cross,
But spear and nails assured His death,
And love's the battle's loss.
But some may say tomorrow holds
The Resurrection Day,
And trusting that, the heart embolds
To keep us in the way.

I stand alone on darkened night
And search the blackened sky
And cannot see, by absent light,
My hand before my eye.
Above my head no star resides
Or beacons yet my feet,
Yet, I must cross a chasm wide
Where earth and heaven meet.
Then, must I know behind the clouds
The heaven's light abides,
And light lives on though darkness shrouds
It from our yearning eyes.

# EVERY DAY IS EASTER DAY

Now that Easter's over and the last lily's gone
And every colored egg is found upon the spacious lawn,
Now that candlestands and crosses on the hill
Have neatly been removed and packed away until
Another day, another time, a year or so from now,
Is Easter really gone or does it live in us somehow?

A stone removed, an empty tomb, some cloth of linen white,
Three women there, amazed, afraid at early morning light,
But that was then, and this is now, another time and place.
And Peter ran, with John ahead, to see the savior's face.
So what of Easter have we left? What Grace remains today?
What clue have we that shows the power, that opens up the Way?

T'was Grace He gave to suffering thief that hung on Calvary hill,
And Grace He gives to you and me, and Grace He always will.
For Grace is gift we don't deserve, a gift we'd never win,
An innocence we can't regain, release from ancient sin.
For God so loved the world He gave his own begotten Son.
In Him did Grace abide, by Him the victory's won.

And everyday is Easter Day, an Easter people, we
When God we seek in fervent prayer, t'is Jesus Christ we see.
When stone was rolled from Garden door, and Jesus stepped outside
He stepped into the hearts of those Who've on His grace relied.
And every day within our hearts the Resurrection yet takes place
And once again our Hope's renewed before the Savior's face.

And when I kneel in private place with broken heart and pray
And Jesus breaks the ancient chains, for me t'is Easter Day.
And every time I've given up, despairing at my pain
He gently lifts my burden and holds me close again.
The stone is gone, the Savior lives, the Life, the Truth, the Way,
And Hope returns for every day we have's another Easter Day.

# PENTECOST

*The fiftieth day after the resurrection: Pentecost!  And the church was born!*

And hidden in an upper room, beyond the city street,
The faithful stayed, believers prayed
In frightened, pained retreat.

And mighty wind with mighty force and fiery sacred heat,
Did hearts consume and fill the room,
Above that city street..

And men fell cold upon the stone or knelt at Jesus' feet
To hear Him say He'd heard them pray
Before the judgement seat.

And fire rained down upon the souls of those who'd felt defeat,
Restored them whole and made them bold,
No more in fear retreat.

And men emboldened by the power returned to city street
To preach the Word that they had heard
Salvation, now complete.

And thousands heard the Word that day, the Word we yet repeat,
For born to Earth, its day of birth,
The Church beyond defeat.

And sing we now upon the earth where East and West do meet,
The gates of hell shall not prevail
Nor quench God's holy heat.

For angels sing and heaven rings through vale and city street
Where prophets preach, believers teach
There stands the church complete.

# ABOUT THE AUTHOR

Renfroe Watson is the third of seven children born to Elizabeth and Renfroe, Sr. From the earliest days he loved the out of doors, counting stars and watching flowers unfold. Growing up in the outskirts of Forsyth, Georgia, provided countless days of hiking in the woods, wading in small creeks, and listening for God's voice in creation.

Renfroe is married to the former Phyllis French, and together they had three children: Fred, Jon and David, their greatest joys.

Upon graduating from Young L.G. Harris College and LaGrange College, Renfroe entered Candler Seminary, Emory University to prepare for Christian ministry, where he has served for more than forty-eight years. For twenty of those years he served in the North Georgia foothills and mountains. For another twenty years, his assignments led him to Atlanta and the surrounding suburbia, with the remaining years divided between Augusta and LaGrange.

Renfroe began writing poetry while a student at Young Harris College where his work often appeared in the campus newspaper. While in Blue Ridge, his work was regularly used during a radio program, "I Walked Where Jesus Walked," and in a weekly column in the city newspaper. Several later works appears appeared in the church's state newspaper. This book, however, is the first attempt to gather and share the writings as a unit.

Renfroe is now retired and living his dream with Phyllis on the property where he grew up. Together, and largely with their own hands, they have built their house and made their home. Today, he may most likely be found working in the yard or rebuilding another old Studebaker (He's currently working on his fifth restoration). And if should one arrive early enough, he may be found sitting, listening and writing in the garden swing from which the works of God are so freshly seen.

Printed in the United States
70788LV00007B/141